Mother's Day Colouring Book

Wonderfully relaxing & calming artwork

First published in 2016 by Clarity Media Ltd
Copyright © Clarity Media Ltd

Illustrations and layout by Amy Smith

Mum...

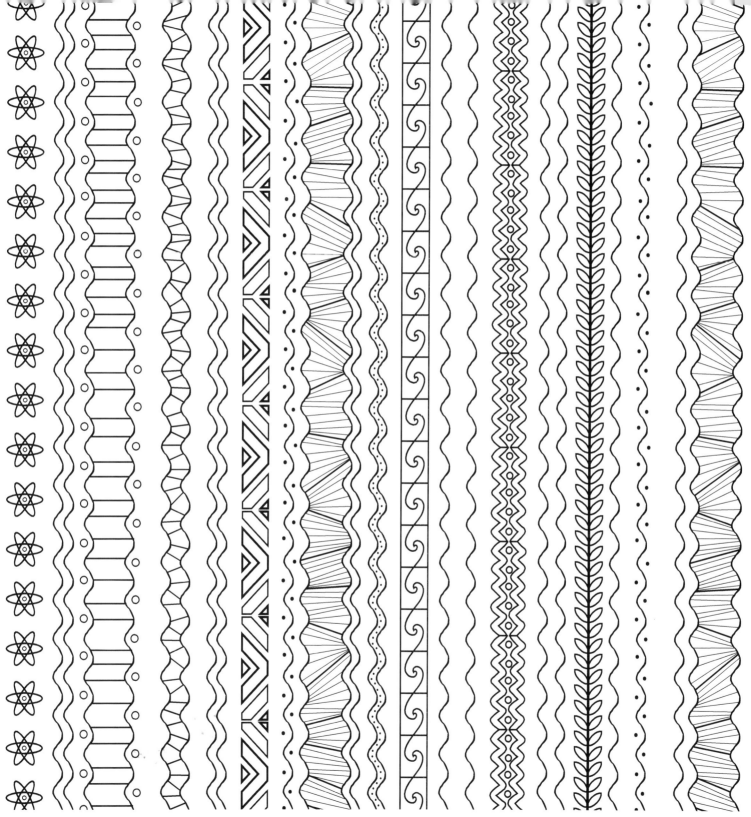

mmmm WONDERFUL
THOUGHTFUL gentle
encouraging KIND patient inspirational
SUPPORTIVE sweet smart love
COMFORTING
giving loyal loving mom
FORGIVING affectionate
protective generous
reliable NURTURING
tender dedicated

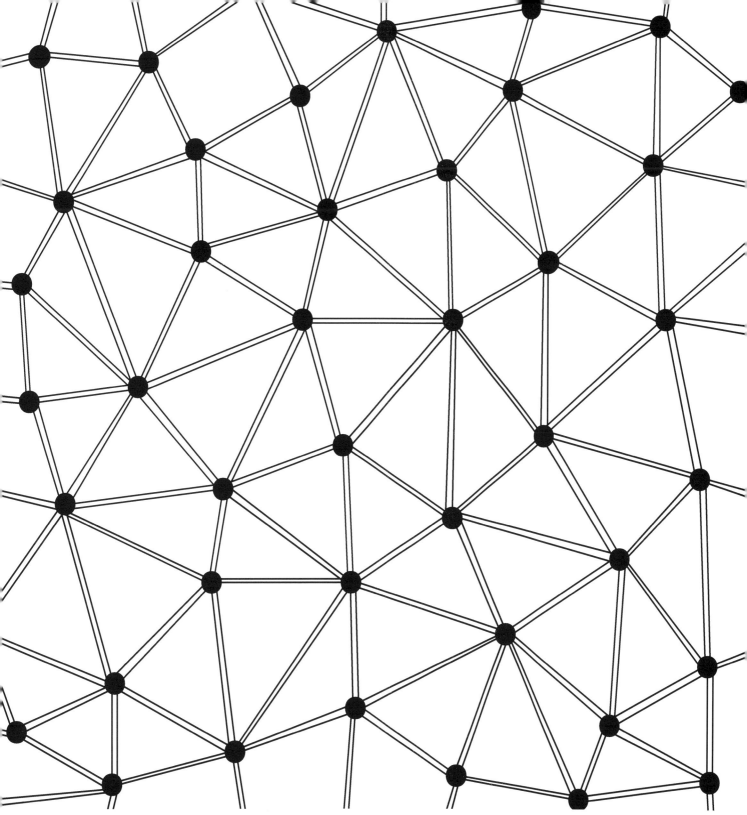

Printed in Great Britain
by Amazon